The No Worries Planner

_____

Emotional Triggers

_____   _____

_____   _____

_____   _____

Physical Triggers

_____   _____

_____   _____

_____   _____

HOW I CAN AVOID TRIGGERS:

I am Stronger Than I think

WHAT I'M STRESSED ABOUT:

_____

_____

_____

_____

WHAT WORRIES ME THE MOST:

_____

_____

_____

_____

WHAT I CAN DO TO MANAGE MY STRESS LEVELS:

_____

_____

_____

_____

Look how Far You've Come...

WRITE ABOUT A TIME IN YOUR LIFE WHERE YOU WERE STRESSED BUT OVERCAME IT:

Breathe in,
Breathe out,

**WHERE DO YOU FIND STRENGTH WHEN
YOU ARE OVERWHELMED?**

Be Your Own Best Friend...

WHAT ADVICE WOULD YOU GIVE A FRIEND WHO WAS FEELING THE WAY YOU ARE?

HOW CAN YOU APPLY THIS ADVICE TO YOUR LIFE?

Managing Difficult Situations

SITUATION:

HOW I FELT:

HOW I COULD HAVE DEALT WITH IT DIFFERENTLY:

Facing Your Fears

WHAT HAVE YOU BEEN AVOIDING?

AVOIDING PROBLEMS NEVER SOLVES THEM. HOW
CAN YOU FACE YOUR FEARS AND OVERCOME
YOUR ANXIETY?:

My Personal Goals

TIME FRAME	WHAT I WANT TO ACCOMPLISH	ACTION PLAN
6 MONTHS		
1 YEAR		
3 YEARS		
5 YEARS		
10 YEARS		

Personal Helpers

ACTIVITIES THAT HELP MANAGE ANXIETY	DATE	✓

Goals for...

DATE:

DATE:

DATE:

DATE:

DATE:

DATE:

This Week's Goals

GOAL	STEPS TO MAKE IT HAPPEN	DATE	✓

GOAL	STEPS TO MAKE IT HAPPEN	DATE	✓

GOAL	STEPS TO MAKE IT HAPPEN	DATE	✓

Weekly Journal

Date: _____

Weekly Check In

DATE

MY THOUGHTS:

SELF CARE CHECKLIST:

HOW I FELT THIS WEEK:

This Week's Goals

GOAL	STEPS TO MAKE IT HAPPEN	DATE	✓

GOAL	STEPS TO MAKE IT HAPPEN	DATE	✓

GOAL	STEPS TO MAKE IT HAPPEN	DATE	✓

Weekly Journal

Date: _____

_____

_____

_____

_____

_____

_____

_____

_____

_____

_____

_____

_____

_____

Weekly Check In

DATE

SELF CARE CHECKLIST:

MY THOUGHTS:

HOW I FELT THIS WEEK:

This Week's Goals

GOAL	STEPS TO MAKE IT HAPPEN	DATE	✓

GOAL	STEPS TO MAKE IT HAPPEN	DATE	✓

GOAL	STEPS TO MAKE IT HAPPEN	DATE	✓

Weekly Journal

Date: _____

Weekly Check In

DATE

MY THOUGHTS:

SELF CARE CHECKLIST:

HOW I FELT THIS WEEK:

This Week's Goals

GOAL	STEPS TO MAKE IT HAPPEN	DATE	✓

GOAL	STEPS TO MAKE IT HAPPEN	DATE	✓

GOAL	STEPS TO MAKE IT HAPPEN	DATE	✓

Weekly Journal

Date: _____

Weekly Check In

DATE

SELF CARE CHECKLIST:

MY THOUGHTS:

HOW I FELT THIS WEEK:

This Week's Goals

GOAL	STEPS TO MAKE IT HAPPEN	DATE	✓

GOAL	STEPS TO MAKE IT HAPPEN	DATE	✓

GOAL	STEPS TO MAKE IT HAPPEN	DATE	✓

Weekly Journal

Date: _____

Weekly Check In

DATE

SELF CARE CHECKLIST:

MY THOUGHTS:

HOW I FELT THIS WEEK:

This Week's Goals

GOAL	STEPS TO MAKE IT HAPPEN	DATE	✓

GOAL	STEPS TO MAKE IT HAPPEN	DATE	✓

GOAL	STEPS TO MAKE IT HAPPEN	DATE	✓

Weekly Journal

Date: _____

_____

_____

_____

_____

_____

_____

_____

_____

_____

_____

_____

_____

_____

Weekly Check In

DATE
_____

SELF CARE CHECKLIST:

MY THOUGHTS:

HOW I FELT THIS WEEK:

This Week's Goals

GOAL	STEPS TO MAKE IT HAPPEN	DATE	✓

GOAL	STEPS TO MAKE IT HAPPEN	DATE	✓

GOAL	STEPS TO MAKE IT HAPPEN	DATE	✓

Weekly Journal

Date: _____

Weekly Check In

DATE

SELF CARE CHECKLIST:

MY THOUGHTS:

HOW I FELT THIS WEEK:

This Week's Goals

GOAL	STEPS TO MAKE IT HAPPEN	DATE	✓

GOAL	STEPS TO MAKE IT HAPPEN	DATE	✓

GOAL	STEPS TO MAKE IT HAPPEN	DATE	✓

Weekly Journal

Date: _____

_____

_____

_____

_____

_____

_____

_____

_____

_____

_____

_____

_____

_____

_____

Weekly Check In

DATE

_____

SELF CARE CHECKLIST:

MY THOUGHTS:

HOW I FELT THIS WEEK:

This Week's Goals

GOAL	STEPS TO MAKE IT HAPPEN	DATE	✓

GOAL	STEPS TO MAKE IT HAPPEN	DATE	✓

GOAL	STEPS TO MAKE IT HAPPEN	DATE	✓

Weekly Journal

Date: _____

Weekly Check In

DATE

SELF CARE CHECKLIST:

MY THOUGHTS:

HOW I FELT THIS WEEK:

This Week's Goals

GOAL	STEPS TO MAKE IT HAPPEN	DATE	✓

GOAL	STEPS TO MAKE IT HAPPEN	DATE	✓

GOAL	STEPS TO MAKE IT HAPPEN	DATE	✓

Weekly Journal

Date: _____

_____

_____

_____

_____

_____

_____

_____

_____

_____

_____

_____

_____

_____

Weekly Check In

DATE

SELF CARE CHECKLIST:

MY THOUGHTS:

HOW I FELT THIS WEEK:

This Week's Goals

GOAL	STEPS TO MAKE IT HAPPEN	DATE	✓

GOAL	STEPS TO MAKE IT HAPPEN	DATE	✓

GOAL	STEPS TO MAKE IT HAPPEN	DATE	✓

Weekly Journal

Date: _____

_____

_____

_____

_____

_____

_____

_____

_____

_____

_____

_____

_____

_____

_____

Weekly Check In

DATE

SELF CARE CHECKLIST:

MY THOUGHTS:

HOW I FELT THIS WEEK:

This Week's Goals

GOAL	STEPS TO MAKE IT HAPPEN	DATE	✓

GOAL	STEPS TO MAKE IT HAPPEN	DATE	✓

GOAL	STEPS TO MAKE IT HAPPEN	DATE	✓

Weekly Journal

Date: _____

_____

_____

_____

_____

_____

_____

_____

_____

_____

_____

_____

_____

_____

Weekly Check In

DATE

_____

MY THOUGHTS:

SELF CARE CHECKLIST:

HOW I FELT THIS WEEK:

This Week's Goals

GOAL	STEPS TO MAKE IT HAPPEN	DATE	✓

GOAL	STEPS TO MAKE IT HAPPEN	DATE	✓

GOAL	STEPS TO MAKE IT HAPPEN	DATE	✓

Weekly Journal

Date: _____

Weekly Check In

DATE

SELF CARE CHECKLIST:

MY THOUGHTS:

HOW I FELT THIS WEEK:

This Week's Goals

GOAL	STEPS TO MAKE IT HAPPEN	DATE	✓

GOAL	STEPS TO MAKE IT HAPPEN	DATE	✓

GOAL	STEPS TO MAKE IT HAPPEN	DATE	✓

Weekly Journal

Date: _____

_____

_____

_____

_____

_____

_____

_____

_____

_____

_____

_____

_____

_____

Weekly Check In

DATE

_____

MY THOUGHTS:

SELF CARE CHECKLIST:

HOW I FELT THIS WEEK:

This Week's Goals

GOAL	STEPS TO MAKE IT HAPPEN	DATE	✓

GOAL	STEPS TO MAKE IT HAPPEN	DATE	✓

GOAL	STEPS TO MAKE IT HAPPEN	DATE	✓

Weekly Journal

Date: ....

Weekly Check In

DATE

SELF CARE CHECKLIST:

MY THOUGHTS:

HOW I FELT THIS WEEK:

This Week's Goals

GOAL	STEPS TO MAKE IT HAPPEN	DATE	✓

GOAL	STEPS TO MAKE IT HAPPEN	DATE	✓

GOAL	STEPS TO MAKE IT HAPPEN	DATE	✓

Weekly Journal

Date: _____

_____

_____

_____

_____

_____

_____

_____

_____

_____

_____

_____

_____

_____

Weekly Check In

DATE

_____

MY THOUGHTS:

SELF CARE CHECKLIST:

HOW I FELT THIS WEEK:

Made in the USA
Columbia, SC
20 August 2023

21887830R00085